# The Nature Kid's Guide to

# ALPACAS

## DAVID ANDERSON

LP Media Inc. Publishing
Text copyright © 2026 by LP Media Inc.


For information address LP Media Inc. Publishing,
30012 Variolite St NW, Princeton MN 55371
www.lpmedia.org

Publication Data

Alpacas
The Nature Kid's Guide to Alpacas — First edition.

Summary: "Learn all about Alpacas, the Nature Kid Way"
— Provided by publisher.

ISBN: 979-8-89818-183-3

[1. Alpacas – Non-Fiction] I. Title.

Title: The Nature Kid's Guide to Alpacas

# CONTENTS

# ALPACA ABODES

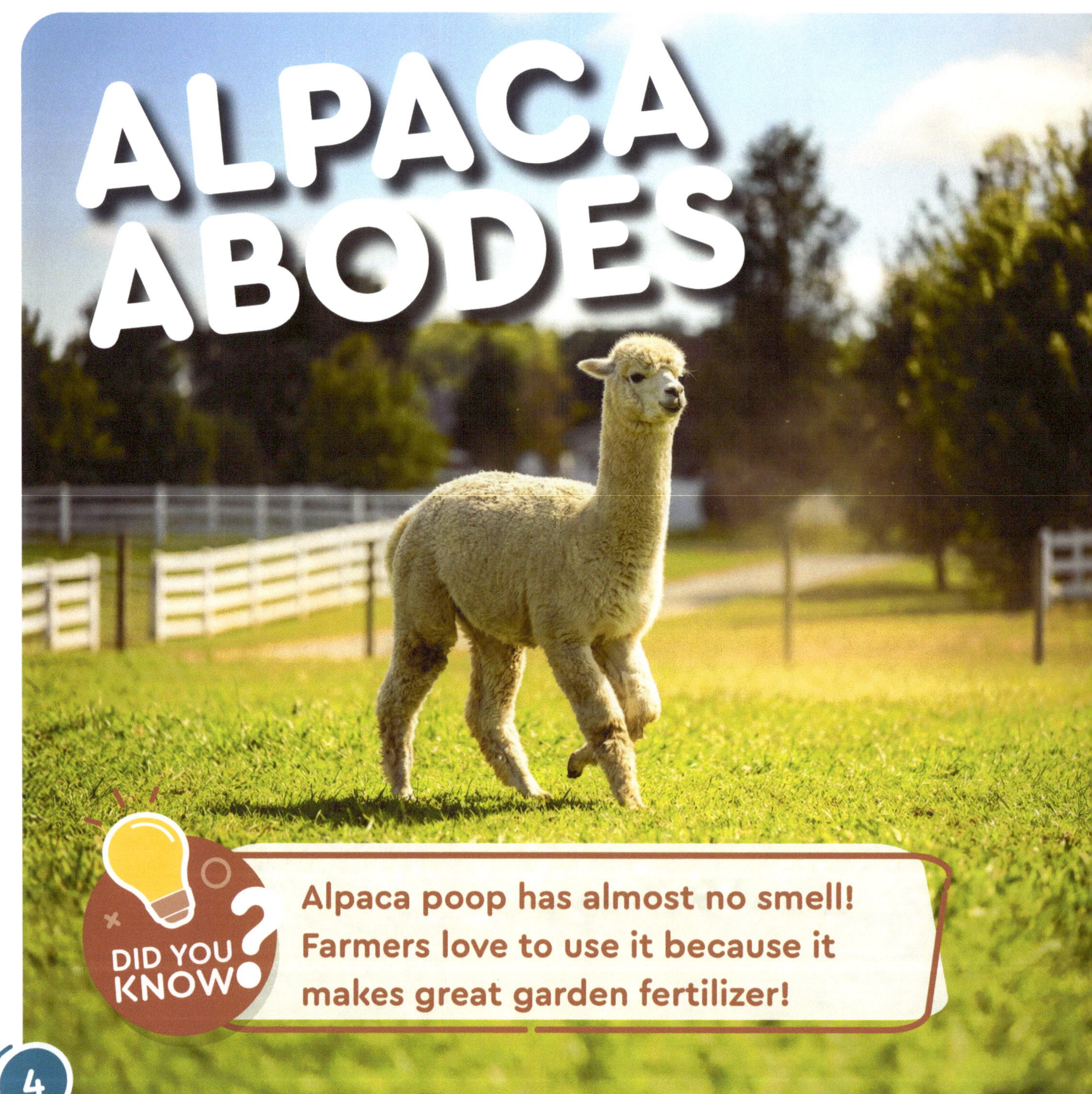



4

**Clip-clop! A fluffy alpaca trots across the sunny green farm.**

Imagine walking into a field and having a fluffy, long-necked animal trot right up to sniff your face. That is what it is like to meet an alpaca! These gentle, curious animals are unlike any other creature on the farm.

Alpacas are not horses, not goats, and not sheep. They are actually related to camels! They come from the high mountains of South America and have been living alongside people for thousands of years.

Today, alpacas are found on farms all over the world. And once you learn what makes them so special, it is easy to see why people everywhere love them.

ANCIENT ANDES
FUN FACT!
Wild vicuñas still roam the Andes — and their fiber is worth more than gold!
6

## Whoosh! A wild vicuña dashes across the tall Andes Mountains.

High in the Andes mountains of South America, the air is thin and the cold can be brutal. Not many animals can survive up there. But the vicuña has for thousands of years.

More than 5,000 years ago, the people of Peru watched these sure-footed wild animals and had an idea. What if they could tame them? Over centuries of careful breeding, the alpaca was born — a domesticated cousin built for farm life rather than wild peaks.

Today the people of Peru treasure alpacas for their incredibly warm **fiber** and their gentle, friendly nature.

# LONG NECKS

FUN FACT!

Alpacas are about half the size of their bigger cousin, the llama!

**Stretch! An alpaca cranes its long neck up high to peek over the fence.**

Alpacas have one feature that makes them stand out in any crowd — that remarkable neck. It can be nearly two feet long, almost a third of their entire height! It helps them reach grass, scan for danger, and get nose to nose with just about anyone they meet.

A grown alpaca stands about three feet tall and weighs around 150 pounds. Their long slender legs look delicate but are surprisingly strong, and their soft padded feet never tear up the grass beneath them.

# FUZZY FEATURES

## Pffft! An alpaca shakes its head and wiggles its long neck.

Alpacas have padded feet with two toes. Their soft, leathery soles do not dig up the ground like horse hooves do, making them one of the most gentle large animals on any farm.

Look at an alpaca's mouth. The top lip is split in two and each side moves on its own! This helps them grab tiny bits of grass with surprising precision. They have teeth only on the bottom jaw — the top is just a hard flat pad for grinding.

Small, pointy ears sit on top of their fuzzy heads and can swivel almost all the way around. Thick fiber covers them from head to toe, keeping them cozy in almost any weather.

# SUPER SENSES

## Swish! An alpaca flicks its ears toward a strange sound.

Alpacas have amazing hearing. Their ears can turn almost all the way around! This helps them pick up sounds from every direction.

Big, dark eyes sit on the sides of their head. Alpacas can see nearly all the way around them without turning. This helps them spot danger fast.

Their nose is powerful too. Alpacas sniff the air to find food and tell who is nearby. They can even recognize other herd members by smell, even in complete darkness!

All these super senses work together to keep the herd safe from harm.

# TWO TYPES

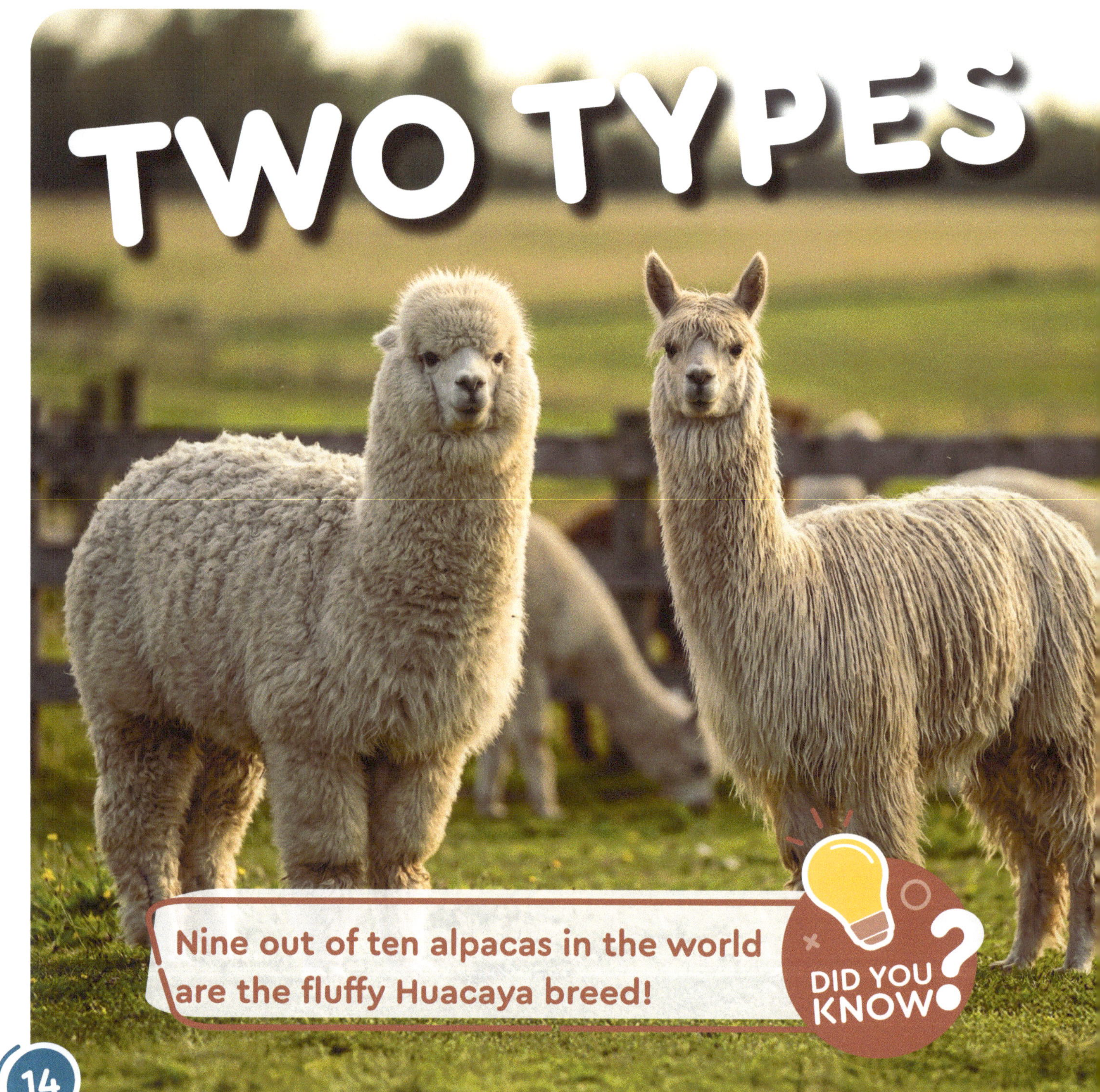

Nine out of ten alpacas in the world
are the fluffy Huacaya breed!

DID YOU
KNOW?

**Baaa! Two alpacas stand side by side but look so different.**

There are two breeds of alpaca. The Huacaya has thick, fluffy fiber that poofs out. It looks like a round, fuzzy cloud!

The Suri breed is different. Its fiber hangs down in long, silky locks. Suris look sleek and wavy — like little rock stars with fancy hairdos!

Alpacas come in more than 20 colors. They can be white, black, brown, gray, or tan. Some even have spots or patches of two colors mixed together. No two alpacas look exactly alike.

# MUNCH TIME

**Crunch! An alpaca bites into a clump of fresh green grass.**

Alpacas are **herbivores**. That means they eat only plants. Grass and hay are their main foods, and they munch on it for hours each day.

Alpacas chew their food twice! First they swallow it quickly. Then it comes back up, and they chew it again slowly. This is called chewing **cud**.

Fresh water is a must every single day. Farmers also give them bits of grain and minerals. This extra food helps alpacas stay healthy and strong.

Alpacas have three stomach parts to break down tough grass — cows have four!

**FUN FACT!**

One alpaca only makes enough fiber each year to knit about four sweaters!

**Buzz! The shearer's clippers glide through thick alpaca fiber.**

Once a year, alpacas get a big haircut! A shearer clips off their thick fiber in about 20 minutes. It does not hurt one bit.

The fiber is very soft and warm. People spin it into yarn, then knit hats, scarves, and cozy sweaters. One alpaca gives about five to ten pounds of fiber each year.

Alpaca fiber is special. It feels light and smooth against the skin. Some people itch in sheep wool but feel great in alpaca fiber. It is also warmer than wool!

# HUMMING ALONG

## Hmmm! A little alpaca hums softly to its mother nearby.

Alpacas talk with sounds. Their most common sound is a gentle hum. They hum when happy, worried, or just curious about something new.

When danger is near, an alpaca makes a loud, sharp cry. It sounds like a high-pitched squeal! The whole herd stops and looks up right away.

Mothers and babies hum to each other all the time. It helps them stay close in a big herd. Alpacas can also cluck, grunt, and even spit when they are angry!

# DAY BY DAY

Alpacas always use one spot as their bathroom — the whole herd shares it!

**Rustle! An alpaca wades through tall grass as the sun comes up.**

Mornings start early for alpacas. As the sun comes up, they walk out to the field and begin munching on grass right away.

By midday, the herd slows down. Alpacas rest in the shade or lie down to soak up the warm sun. Some even take short naps!

As evening comes, they graze one more time before dark. When night falls, alpacas huddle near the barn. They rest close together, keeping each other safe until morning.

PRANCING PALS

DID YOU KNOW?
Alpacas can sprint up to 35 miles per hour — not bad for an animal that spends most of its day eating grass!

**Boing! A young alpaca bounces through the field with glee.**

Alpacas walk in a special way. Both legs on the same side move at once! This gives them a smooth, swaying step.

When alpacas get excited, they **pronk**! They leap into the air with all four feet off the ground. It looks silly and joyful — like a fuzzy bouncing ball.

Alpacas can also run fast when they need to. They zip across a field to escape danger in a flash. But most of the time, they just walk slowly and graze in peace.

# DUST BATHS

Alpacas pick one or two favorite dust bath spots — and the whole herd shares them!

**Poof! An alpaca flops down and rolls in a patch of dry dust.**

Alpacas love dust baths! They find a dry, dusty spot and flop right down. Then they wiggle and roll on their backs with their legs in the air.

The dust helps clean their coat. It soaks up oil and keeps pesky bugs away. It is like nature's own shampoo!

After a good roll, the alpaca stands up and shakes off. A big cloud of dust flies everywhere! Then it walks away looking fresh, clean, and very pleased with itself.

# HERD HANGOUT

At night, alpacas all lie down facing the same direction — nobody in the herd sleeps alone!

**Maaa! A group of alpacas huddles close to stay warm at dawn.**

Alpacas are herd animals. They do not like to be alone — ever! A herd can have just three alpacas or more than twenty.

Every herd has a leader. The leader watches for danger and gets to eat first. The other alpacas follow along and trust the leader's choices.

Alpacas stand or lie down close to each other. They feel safe in a group. If one alpaca is taken away, it gets very sad and may stop eating. These are animals that truly need their friends!

# BABY BOOM

The name 'cria' comes from a Spanish word meaning 'baby' or 'to raise'!

**Squeal! A young cria stands up on a warm spring morning.**

Baby alpacas are called **crias**. A mother is pregnant with her cria for about 11 months. That is almost a whole year of waiting!

Most crias are born in the morning. The warm sunlight helps them dry off and grow strong fast. Mothers almost always have just one baby at a time.

When a birth happens, the herd gathers close. They watch and wait together. It is a big day on the farm — a new fuzzy friend has arrived!

# CUTE CRIAS

DID YOU KNOW?
Crias can tell their own mother apart from other alpacas just by her hum!

**Thump! A tiny cria stands on its wobbly legs for the first time.**

A newborn cria weighs about 15 to 20 pounds. That is about the size of a small dog! It is covered in a damp, fuzzy coat.

Within one hour, the cria stands up. Its legs shake and wobble at first. But soon it takes its very first steps toward its mother!

Crias are very curious little explorers. They love to sniff everything and run in quick little bursts. They bounce and play with other babies in the herd. Baby alpacas are some of the cutest animals on Earth!

# MAMA KNOWS



34

**Sniff! A mother alpaca gently nuzzles her brand-new cria.**

A new cria has just been born. Its mama sniffs it all over carefully. This is how she learns its special scent. She will always know her baby from then on.

The cria drinks its mother's milk many times a day. The rich milk helps the baby grow big and strong quickly. Crias nurse for about six months.

Mothers keep their crias close day and night. They walk side by side wherever they go. A mama alpaca is a caring, watchful parent who never lets her baby out of sight.

GUARD DUTY
DID YOU KNOW?
Some brave guard alpacas have even chased away bears to protect their flock!

**Screech! An alpaca sounds a loud alarm to scare off a fox.**

Some farmers keep alpacas to guard other animals. Alpacas are brave and always alert. They watch over sheep, goats, and even chickens.

If a fox or coyote comes near, the alpaca stands tall. It stamps its feet hard and makes a sharp, loud cry. Most predators turn and run away fast!

Alpacas do not need any training for this job. They guard by instinct — it comes naturally. Just one or two alpacas can protect a whole flock of sheep.

# FUZZY FRIENDS

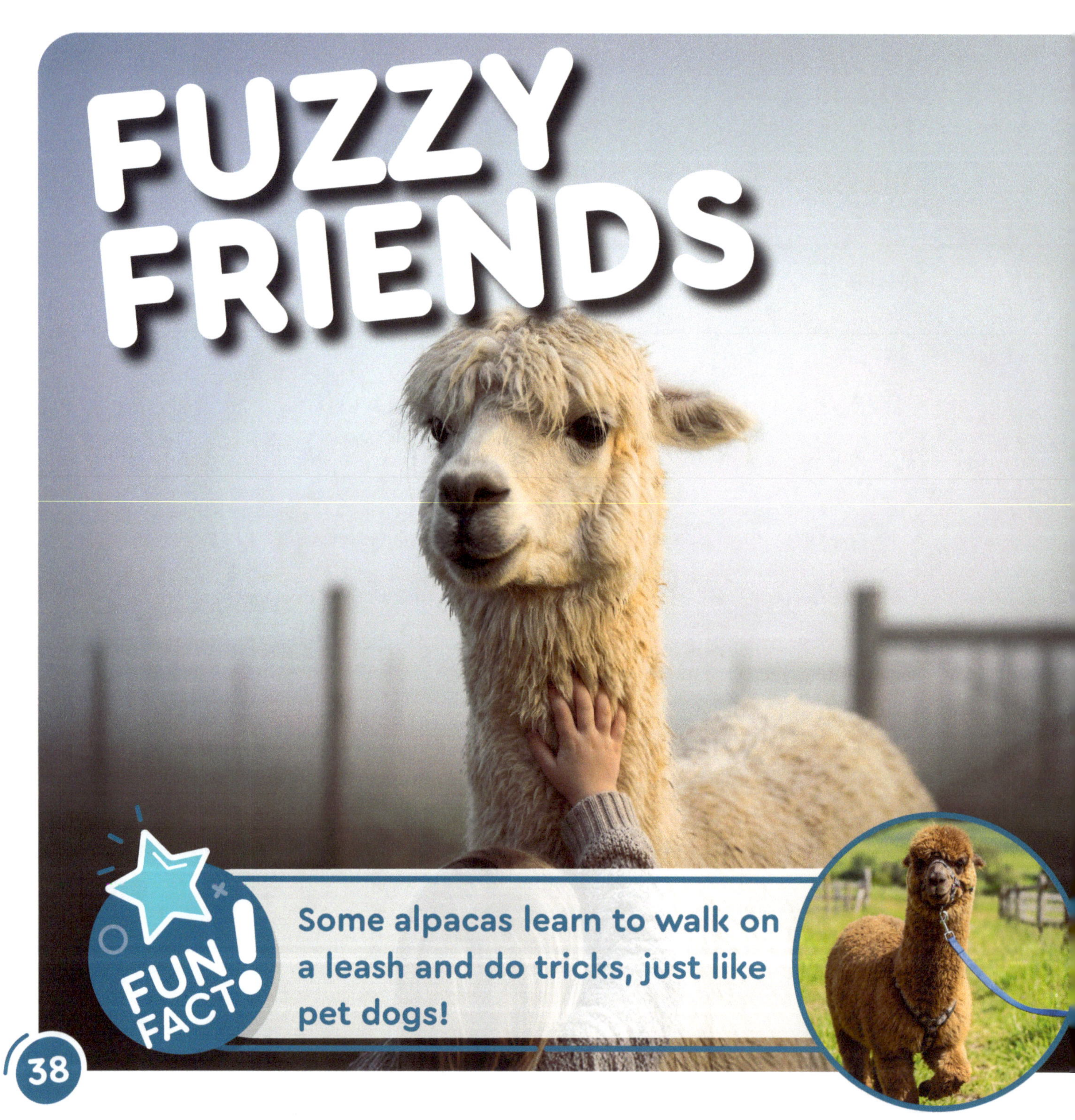



Some alpacas learn to walk on a leash and do tricks, just like pet dogs!

## Pat-pat! A calm alpaca leans in as a child pets its warm neck.

Alpacas and people have been friends for thousands of years. Today, many farms let visitors come meet the alpacas up close.

Alpacas are sweet and calm around people. Some visit schools and hospitals as therapy animals. A quiet alpaca can make a sad day feel so much better.

Taking care of alpacas teaches kids about kindness and responsibility. These fuzzy friends give us warm fiber, joyful fun, and gentle love. No wonder so many people around the world adore them!

# GLOSSARY

**cria**

A baby alpaca

**cud**

Food that comes back up
to be chewed again

**fiber**

The hair that grows on an
alpaca's body

**pronk**

A joyful leap into the air
with all four feet off the
ground at once!

**herbivore**

An animal that eats only
plants

www.ingramcontent.com/pod-product-compliance
Lightning Source LLC
Chambersburg PA
CBHW041608110726
48005CB00002B/334